'The Big Reconnecting Self-Love Journal' is full of prompts and affirmations to remind you to love and connect with your Self as Allah has made you a unique individual with incredible strengths and talents to use in this life, benefiting yourself and others. Please savour the lists, returning to them from time to time making them long and rich, a full reflection of you.

Originally these prompts were crafted for the adventurous, fitra-healing sisters who join Khalida Haque and Brooke Benoit at The Big Reconnect Sleepover, a retreat in Morocco exclusively for Muslim women. We are so pleased that Stori Dori appreciates our work enough that they have chosen to release our journal as part of their Collaborative Signatures Collection.

To find out more about our retreats in Morocco and the UK, please visit thebigreconnectsleepover.com.

For more gorgeous life planning and improving tools, please visit storidori.com.

Please find us on our social media, we'd love to hear about (and see) your discoveries and growth using 'The Big Reconnecting Self-Love Journal.'

www.instagram.com/thebigreconnectsleepover
www.facebook.com/fikranddhikrbooks/

I love myself, as Allah loves me

List
EVERYTHING I LOVE ABOUT MYSELF.

Struggling with this one? What compliments have others given you? What have others said that they like about you?

> "I wish I could show you, when you are lonely or in darkness, the astonishing light of your own being." — HAFIZ OF SHIRAZ

Love Prompt
CRAFT YOUR IDEAL DEFINITIONS OF FREEDOM, LOVE, AND HAPPINESS

"Self-compassion is simply giving the same kindness to ourselves that we would give to others." - CHRISTOPHER GERMER

List
EVERYTHING I WANT TO SAY "YES!" TO

Include things that seem impossible, far-fetched and downright crazy. List with full abandon.

"When you have confidence, you can have a lot of fun. And when you have fun, you can do amazing things." - JOE NAMATH

List
EVERYTHING I WANT TO SAY "NO," TO

Everything and anything that you would say no to if you weren't afraid.

"If you want to sing out, sing out, and if you want to be free, be free, cause there's a million ways to be, you know that there are."

- YUSUF ISLAM

Love Prompt
WHO AM I? AND WHAT IS MY INDIVIDUAL MEANING AND PURPOSE?

If you're struggling to think of anything, think back to the time you were still firmly in touch with your fitra, (7-14 years old). What did you enjoy doing, what were your hopes and aspirations, what were you good at and who/what did you want to become?

"What in your life is calling you? When all the noise is silenced, the meetings adjourned, the lists laid aside, and the wild iris blooms by itself in the dark forest, what still pulls on your soul? In the silence between your heartbeats hides a summons, do you hear it? Name it, if you must, or leave it forever nameless, but why pretend it is not there?" - THE TERMA COLLECTIVE

> "Everyone has been made for some particular work, and the desire for that work has been put in every heart." - RUMI

"Self-care is never a selfish act – it is simply good stewardship of the only gift I have, the gift I was put on earth to offer to others."
- PARKER PALMER

List

ALL THE THINGS I HAVE ACCOMPLISHED

Include things that you have overcome, any difficulties or flaws as well as achievements such as qualifications and skills learnt.

Love Prompt

WRITE A LETTER TO YOUR YOUNGER SELF THANKING HER FOR SOME CHOICES SHE MADE OR ACTIONS SHE TOOK THAT YOU CAN APPRECIATE THE FRUITS OF TODAY.

"Acquire wisdom from the story of those who have already passed."
- UTHMAN IBN AFFAN (RA)

List
EVERYTHING EVER I AM THANKFUL FOR

"If patience and gratitude had been she camels, it would have mattered little on which I rode." - UMAR IBN AL KHATTAB (RA)

> "Gratitude unlocks the fullness of life. It turns what we have into enough, and more. It turns denial into acceptance, chaos to order, confusion to clarity. It can turn a meal into a feast, a house into a home, a stranger into a friend. Gratitude makes sense of our past, brings peace for today and creates a vision for tomorrow."
> – MELODY BEATTIE

List
MY FAVORITE COMFORTING VERSES FROM THE QU'RAN OR HADITH

"[This is] a blessed Book which We have revealed to you, [O Muhammad], that they might reflect upon its verses and that those of understanding would be reminded." - (SAAD: 29)

List

EVERYTHING I THINK IS SUBHAN ALLAH BEAUTIFUL

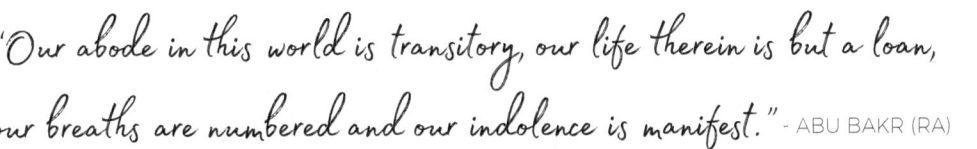

"Our abode in this world is transitory, our life therein is but a loan, our breaths are numbered and our indolence is manifest." - ABU BAKR (RA)

"We delight in the beauty of the butterfly but rarely admit the changes it has gone through to achieve that beauty." — MAYA ANGELOU

Love Prompt

WHEN DID I START TO LOSE MY SENSE OF SELF? WHEN DID I RECOGNISE THAT I DIDN'T KNOW WHO I WAS?

"Stop trying to be less of who you are. Let this time in your life cut you open and drain all of the things that are holding you back."
- JENNIFER ELISABETH

Love Prompt

WRITE TO YOUR YOUNGER SELF AND PROVIDE HER WITH SOME MUCH NEEDED PRAISE BUT ALSO SOME CONSTRUCTIVE FEEDBACK AS TO WHAT SHE COULD HAVE DONE BETTER.

"Your pain is the breaking of the shell that encloses your understanding" - KHALIL GIBRAN

List

MY PAINS, MY BURDENS AND MY HARDSHIPS - SO THAT YOU MAY ACKNOWLEDGE THAT THIS LIFE ISN'T EASY

"What lies behind us and what lies before us are tiny matters compared to what lies within us." - RALPH WALDO EMERSON

"There is a gulf of difference between doing something for self absorbed, narcissistic personal gain and doing something that allows us to recharge, replenish and feel human once more." - KHALIDA HAQUE

Love Prompt
IMAGINE THAT YOU ARE FULLY FEARLESS. WHAT THINGS MIGHT YOU DO?

"The learned lives although he dies." - ALI IBN ABU TALIB (RA)

Love Prompt

WHAT DO I WANT TO BE REMEMBERED FOR? WHAT DO I WANT PEOPLE TO SAY ABOUT ME UPON HEARING OF MY DEATH? #LEGACY

"Love yourself. Love others. Just love. Love makes everything easier."
- KHALIDA HAQUE

All rights reserved 2017 © Stori Dori & The Big Reconnect Sleepover.

For individual private use only. No part of this book may be reproduced or transmitted in any form or by any means - electronic, mechanical, photocopying, recording or otherwise - without prior permission of Stori Dori and The Big Reconnect Sleepover.

46° Collab 2017.
Designed by reyoflightdesign.com.

www.ingramcontent.com/pod-product-compliance
Lightning Source LLC
Chambersburg PA
CBHW070545300426
44113CB00011B/1798